Rottweilers

Dog Books for Kids

By
K. Bennett

Mendon Cottage Books

JD-Biz Publishing

Read More Amazing Animal Books

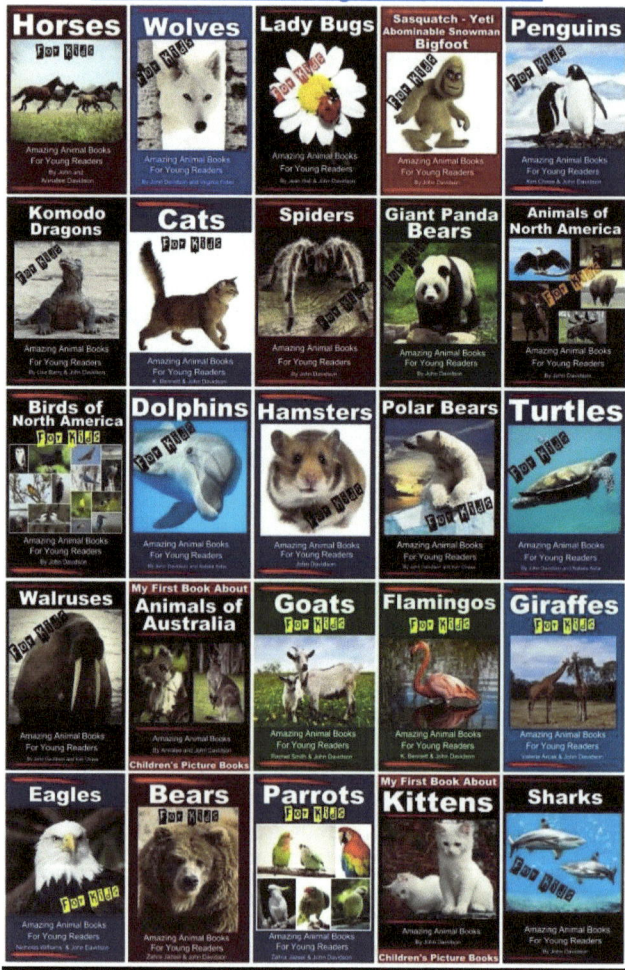

Purchase at Amazon.com

Table of Contents

Introduction

"No matter how little money and how few possessions you own, having a dog makes you rich."

— *Louis Sabin*

Rottweilers are powerful dogs from a long history of domestic dogs, also known as butchers dogs. Strong, courageous and intelligent,

Rottweilers are versatile and faithful dogs. They have outstanding characteristics and are devoted to their family.

Butchers dogs were used to herd livestock in Germany. Do you know why the name "butcher" was used? The carts were full of "butchered" meat and other products to sell. So, when the dogs pulled the carts they were called "butchers" dogs.

Today, Rottweilers are found not only at home, but also in law enforcement. They form a part of search and rescue teams and help the blind as guide dogs. This ability extends to work as police dogs and guard dogs.

The AKC standard defines Rottweilers as "calm and confident." They also note a "self-assured aloofness that does not lend itself to immediate and indiscriminate friendships." This statement helps us to understand the level of socialization required for a Rottweiler. It also helps us to learn how much training is needed for a friendlier, more outgoing pet.

Rottweilers are excellent watchdogs and guardians. Their alert and protective nature can serve to protect both you and your family from strangers. However, like other dog breeds, this aspect of their personality may not appeal to you, if you are looking for a more guest friendly dog.

This breed has a high energy level and strong territorial instincts, which are other aspects to consider. A slow lifestyle is not ideal, as they have a tendency to get a bit overweight. For this reason, they require daily exercise and space to expend that energy. Mental exercise is another very important factor to take into account.

Despite their strong personality and characteristics, Rottweilers are highly recommended as guardians and protectors. With proper training and firm attention, Rottweilers make an excellent addition to the list of … *man's best friend*!

When I get bored, I get creative!

 # Chapter 1

An interesting start – Roman Empire

Rottweilers have an interesting history dating back many years. It goes as far back as the Roman Empire when Romans used drover dogs.

Drovers were powerful dogs with great guarding instincts. They traveled the land along with their owners helping keep the cattle together and well protected.

Romans did not have refrigerators at the time, and brought their "food" along with them. In the case of cattle, Romans used drover dogs to keep the cattle in one place so they would not scatter across the countryside. They also used drover dogs to protect the herds at night.

During their travels, Romans travelled into the area known as Southern Germany today. After a while, a town in this area got the name Rottweil. This area was very important in trade, and the descendants of the drover dogs proved their skills by safeguarding the herds from wild animals and robbers.

During the middle ages, the dogs came to be known by the name butcher dogs, and they helped many traveling butchers make it safely to the market. However, when the railroads became the most important way to take cattle stock to the market, butcher dogs lost their popularity.

The arrival of World War I and the need for police and guard dogs was a major boost for this breed. Soon Rottweilers were serving their owners as guard dogs, ambulance dogs, and even messenger dogs!

To think about: Some Rottweilers have strong personalities. And if they do not receive the proper socialization at an early age, this dominant personality could be tiresome over the years. For this reason, it is important to get the proper training skills. And you may need a professional to help you in this regard.

Note of advice: Rottweilers are not recommended for first time dog owners due to their strong nature.

In training mode

A dog by any other name…

Remember: Rottweilers are high energy dogs, so they need a lot of space and activities to keep them occupied. Bu,t they are also trainable, so you can help your dog understand commands and when ***not*** to do something!

Mentally, the dog requires training as well. And with this breed mental training is very important. Why? This breed is inclined towards dominance. Of course this may not apply to your pet and there are exceptions to the rule. However, for the most part, Rottweilers tend to dominate their living area.

This personality can reflect in territorial instincts and inclination to control their surroundings. This basically means "they" will tell "you" *what* to do and *when* to do it! So mental training is a must.

What is the difference from physical training? As noted previously, if you do not prove you are the "leader," your dog may take over for you. And Rottweilers can find creative ways to let you know when you are not in control. They may act a bit more aggressive than you would like and may even bark or growl.

In some extreme cases this can include unstable tempers or overaggressive behavior. Of course, we do not want to get to these extremes so, take care to handle both aspects of the training from an early age.

If you are unable to handle these requirements, please get the help of a professional trainer. Choose your trainer wisely. Remember you are training with love and affection, so choose someone who understands these important qualities and will handle your pet as you would yourself.

Strong & Steady

 **Chapter 2**

Now that you know what a Rottweiler's personality is like and where it came from, let us examine some of its features:

In review: Rottweilers are likely descended from drover dogs. They are versatile and have been around for a long time. Although called *butchers dogs* for their skills, today we know this breed as a Rottweiler.

They also possess great guarding skills and will defend their home. Because of these great qualities, over the years they have assisted police and law enforcement to do their jobs.

They also make excellent guardians, and are a great asset if protection is important to you.

FUN FACTS FOR KIDS: Did you know the standard Rottweiler has a colored dot above each eye? Check out the inner brow ridge of the eye to find markings. What color is it? Be sure to ask your parents or a guardian's permission before you do!

- *How much can they weigh?* The male can weigh approximately 110-130 pounds, and the female can weigh approximately 77-106 pounds. This doesn't mean a Rottweiler can't weigh more / less than this, but this is the standard weight.

-*How tall can they get?* A male can reach 24 – 27 inches in height, and a female can get to 22 – 25 inches in height.

-*What about babies?* Rottweiler's litters are large. And the female can have between 8 – 12 puppies.

-*How long to they live?* Lifespan is usually between 8 - 10 years.

-*What about their coat?* They have a double coat. It is thick and hard with short hair. Properly groomed, it will be glossy and easy to care for.

-*How often do they shed?* Normally, before they are in season, the coat will shed a great deal. If you suffer from allergies, this is something to consider.

-*What color are they?* Rottweilers are beautiful dogs with a distinctive look. Unlike other dog breeds, their coat is a typical black with mahogany or rust colored markings. The markings are located in specific areas from the ridge of the eye to the side of the snout, throat and chest, under the tail and down the legs. The markings on the coat are quite artistic and appealing to many owners.

- *What about their temperament or personality?* Rottweilers are confident and steady dogs. As we have discussed, they are highly athletic and energetic. They are also alert, noble and self-assured. This part of their personality is very noticeable in the bearing of the breed.

Rottweilers are highly protective of their home and the environment around them. This alert nature helps them develop as excellent guard dogs, and any suspicious activity will result in action. It is important to note this breed will attack if needed. Their overprotective or aggressive nature can kick in quite strongly, and they will do whatever is necessary.

If you wish to get a Rottweiler, please remember this aspect of their personality. And the most important part: Start from young (puppy) if you can. DO NOT just get any dog that crosses your path. The right breeder is important to ensure a well behaved and socialized pet.

Note: A breeder may not be available in your community or a puppy may not be an option. If an adult dog is your choice, choose a nice shelter or rescue organization. Ask them for a Rottweiler with a good personality and few negative traits.

Rottweiler in natural background

Caring for your Rottweiler

Rottweilers are valued members of a home, so we want to be sure they get proper care. And like most, if not all of us, the right diet and exercise is important.

Let us begin with the right diet: Gauging how much your dog should eat is a good place to start. If you notice your pet may be getting a little too heavy, cut back on the food intake. If you notice too little weight, then increase the portions of food.

Gauging your pet's nutritious needs is an important step for this breed. Rottweilers tend to get overweight if not fed correctly. This can lead to obesity and seriously affect the health of your pet. So how can you be sure if your dog is being fed correctly?

The same principle applies for other breeds, but this general rule of thumb is a nice way to test your animal to see how well you are feeding him.

Try the following test listed on **dogtime.com** at home. Are you ready?

FIRST: Put your thumbs on his spine and run your fingers along the side of the Rottweiler's body.

SECOND: Once there, feel for his ribs beneath the muscle. If you can see them, he needs more food! If you cannot feel them (Too many rolls of fat), you need to put him / her on a diet.

This other test comes from **Rottrescue.org**. They recommend the following step:

Have your dog stand up and give them a good look. Does your dog have the same width from shoulders to hips? Can you see a "waist" anywhere? It should be DISTINCT and noticeable. If you are unable to tell where the waist, shoulders and hips start and stop...you get the idea!

These two simple tests will help you feed your dog in the correct manner.

Mealtime

Rottweilerhq.com notes the following meal suggestions for your pet:
An adult dog should have 22 – 26% protein in their diet. A puppy
should have 24 – 28 % protein in their diet.

Fat content should be 12 – 16% for an adult and 14 – 18% for a puppy.
No chemical preservatives, artificial color or sugar.

Remember… a great diet will go a long way to a healthy and happy
pet!

Now on to exercises: Remember: exercise is important to this breed,
and this can include:

-Break a sweat

Rottweilers need exercise and lots of it. So you can jog, run or walk
briskly to get their blood flowing. (Note: This is a daily requirement, so
if you unable to meet this type of demand on your time, a Rottweiler
may not be the ideal pet for you)

-Socializing

Socialization is incredibly important for this breed. So take the time to introduce your pet to other animals and people as well. If you are walking in a park or other social area, stop for a moment and help your dog to know it is all right to meet others. Take note if your pet seems uncomfortable with this due to their suspicious nature, and take it one step at a time.

-Running

(Try to stay away from really hard surfaces. An open field (park area or similar site) is better for its low impact on the frame of your pet. This will help their joints and feet to keep in tip top shape.)

Running in the water

Living with the family

Exposing your Rottweiler to children and other animals in the home at a young age is an excellent start. Rottweilers are great playmates for children and will interact well with other family pets IF, and only IF, they have been socialized well.

Leadership is another important step for this breed. Once you take the lead the dog will follow. They thrive on a pack relationship with you, the owner, as the head pack leader. It is important to know this relationship must be ongoing and consistent. Then everyone will be happy!

However, if you are hesitant and unsure about these important steps, talk to a reputable Veterinarian or professional trainer for more tips on what to do.

Little girl with two Rottweilers – Sharing a happy time

🐾 Chapter 3

Happy face

Keeping it effective

This online article (Training Rottweilers) encourages the following ways to train your pet. This training method applies for other breeds as well and has been listed in previous books. However, this same principle applies to Rottweilers and should be noted.

1- ***Make it about them and not you***. This training skill is interesting and should be considered. Michele Welton from the website '***your pure*** *bread puppy'* notes that training should be about the DOG and not about YOU.

The "positive only" dog training (Which includes a clicker) is something rather common today. This is where you reward the dog for doing something you ask / need it to do. In other words you bribe it to death!

She does not recommend this procedure for the simple reason that it alludes to "operant conditioning." For the dog to act, it will listen for the clicker and respond. But if you do not have a clicker, will the dog *really* obey you? Good question, right?

So make the training about your DOG. What it needs, desires, wants, etc., not what you feel it should be. After all, we want our dogs to be individual creatures with their own funny quirks, styles and actions.

Of course, the above advice does not mean you will not train your pet. It only means you will train it in the right way.

2 – *Try* **RESPECT TRAINING** *instead.* This is where you actually teach your animal to learn from **POSITIVE** and **NEGATIVE** consequences.

As a human we also learn from these same principles. For example: If we do something for someone and they say thank you, we may do it again. And yet if we forget to take out the garbage, and Daddy blows his top, more than likely we will not do it again. (At least we hope!)

Dogs, and in this case Rottweilers, learn in the same way. If our pet does something great we can reward it with smiles, hugs, laughs, kisses, games, treats, and whatever other happy outcome you will like.

On the other hand, if our pet does something we do not like we can transmit that with our voice, our look or use the leash or collar. It is important to note you will not hit, kick or otherwise abuse the animal. A simple tug with a firm voice is usually enough for the animal to figure out something is off.

This dignifies the dog and teaches it both respect and appreciation for boundaries. With loving attention and care, you can have a happy, obedient pet and a happy home.

A word of caution to this tale…

Rottweilers do not have the best reputation, and their exceptional strength and aggression has created a perception that goes a long way. Many people fear this breed and others consider them too dangerous to have around.

It is important to note a healthy degree of respect for this dog. And it is true their personality is not to be taken lightly. If you do decide to make Rottweilers a part of your family, it is important to remember these negative factors that could impact your pet:

-Neglect
-No socialization
-Abuse
-Lack of training
-Irresponsible ownership

This list contributes to an unstable pet. If you decide to get an adult Rottweiler, be sure these factors were not a part of the dog's early days.

Of course, there are many stories of goofy, kindhearted and loving Rottweilers that fill many homes and delight the hearts of their families. But weighing the pros and cons of any pet is a healthy way to ensure successful ownership!

So, what else can we learn about Rottweilers? Check out some amazing facts you may like to know!

- Rottweilers have a noble personality. They are territorial, generally aloof and do not take kindly to strangers invading their space.

However, if you properly socialize the dog and train them well, they will be better equipped to deal with people they do not know.

- If they sense you / your family is in danger, they will act. Their protective skills kick in and they can let out a ferocious bark, or even attack! They are not fearful and will not hesitate to jump into a dangerous situation.

- They have a lot of energy to release, so you need an active lifestyle to keep up with them. They do not do well being left on their own and can get easily get depressed. This depressive behavior can turn destructive, so keep up healthy activities and your pet will thank you!

- Rottweilers have a "wait and see" personality. If they "see" something they stand guard ready to act. It is important to channel this energy in the right way, so your pet can distinguish friend from foe.

- Rottweilers thrive on leadership and want you to take charge! If you lead them well, they will respond with loyal affection. And if you love them, they will surely love you in return, and will not hesitate to show that love throughout their lifetime

So much fun!

FUN FACTS FOR KIDS: Rottweilers are called ***Rottweiler Metzgerhund*** in the German language. Their nicknames are Rott and Rottie for short, and they have been around for a long time. How long? Wikipedia says their history likely dates back to the days of the Roman Empire, when drover dogs were used to herd and drive cattle. Do you know when the Roman Empire existed? As your parent or guardian to help you find the answer in a history book or online!

 Conclusion

A boy's best friend too!

In conclusion:

Rottweilers are great dogs, and a protective addition to any home. As ideal guardians, their protective instincts are hard to beat. And they are intelligent, noble and eager to please you.

Their skills do not extend only to the home but outdoors as well. Even the police and the military use this dog to help track down individuals who break the law.

It is true their protective or overprotective nature may get them into trouble. It is also true 'this breed walks a fine line between protectiveness and aggressiveness', as noted at **dogtime.com**. But accept it as another outstanding quality of this beautiful dog.

And if they seem more overbearing than you would like, consider this an alert to help them use that pent up energy in a more productive way.

Ultimately, Rottweilers are not only man's best friend, but a family friend too! So, if you decide to make this breed a part of your family home, you could not make a better choice than a steady, courageous and loyal companion.

Author Bio

K. Bennett is a native from the Island of Roatan, North of Honduras. She loves to write about many different subjects, but writing for children is special to her heart.

Some of her favorite pastimes are reading, traveling and discovering new things. These activities help to fuel her imagination and act like a canvas for more stories.

She also loves fantasy elements like hidden worlds and faraway lands. Basically anything that gets her imagination soaring to new heights!

Her writing credits include local newspaper articles, a writing blog at Wordpress.com and other online stories. It also includes nonfiction books, children books online, and two novellas listed on Amazon.com

Our books are available at
1. Amazon.com

2. Barnes and Noble

3. Itunes

4. Kobo

5. Smashwords

6. Google Play Books

This book is published by

JD-Biz Corp

P O Box 374

Mendon, Utah 84325

http://www.jd-biz.com/

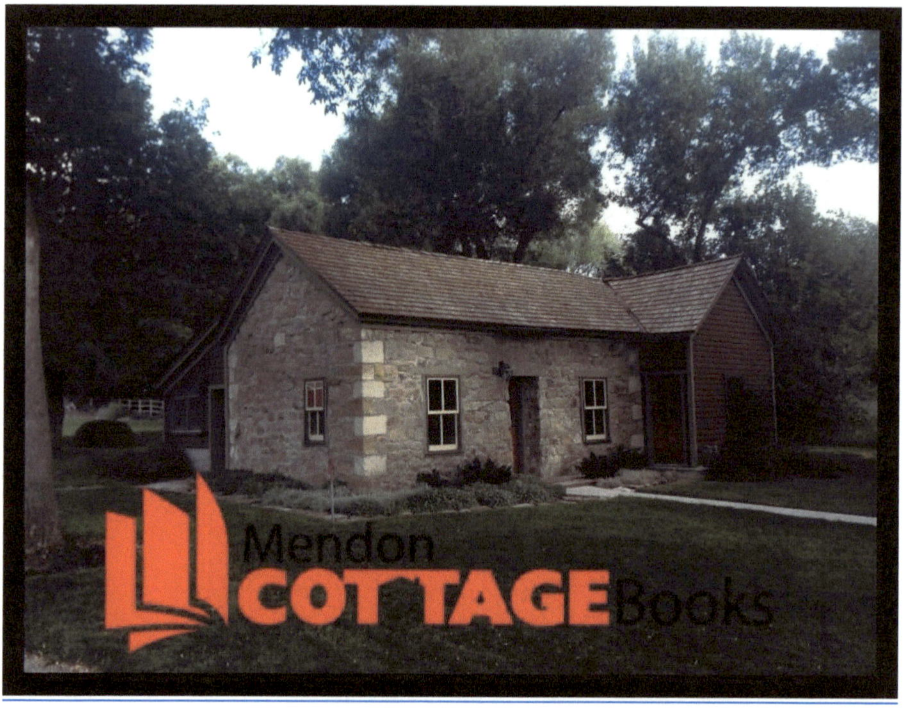

CPSIA information can be obtained
at www.ICGtesting.com
Printed in the USA
BVHW021201201218
536083BV00005B/270/P

9 781517 108885